Printed in the USA by A2Z Books, LLC.

Copyright 2021 Carolyn Blake
All rights reserved.

This book or any portion thereof may
not be reproduced or used in any manner whatsoever without the
express written permission of the publisher except
for the use of brief quotations in book review.

Printed in the United States.
First Printing
ISBN 978-1-955148-27-6
www.A2ZBookspublishing.net

This Healing Journal

Belongs to:

_____

_____

Unspoken Hurt – Heart Healing

Psalm 27: *The Lord is my light and my salvation; whom shall I fear? The Lord is the strength of my life; of whom shall I be afraid?*

Have you ever been hurt? I mean really hurt to the core of your heart, but you never spoke about it. It's called unspoken hurt. A hurt that you left unattended, unnurtured, and dormant. A heart hurt that you thought would never go away or be healed. You do this and the other but find no peace, no fulfillment, and no real true joy.

Well, I've had many of those unspoken hurt episodes in my lifetime, and it almost destroyed my livelihood, my independence, my emotional stability, and my self-esteem. I Couldn't Hear Me Cry. I Couldn't Hear Me Cry for the things that wanted to come to the surface and be dealt with; I couldn't hear me cry because I wanted to forgive and be forgiven. I couldn't hear me cry because that little girl didn't want to remember the unspoken hurt. Maybe you are one of those men or women that have done or are still doing this afraid to unleash the hurt, confess the sin, forgive those that hurt you or even forgive yourself.

You've been impacted and continue to let the unspoken heart hurts imprison and hold you in bondage. In this writing, I will be sharing some unspoken heart hurts that I overcame and some I'm still working on, but I at least want to help you get to heart healing so you will be able to function in some normalcy because you've decided to take action and find wholeness through brokenness.

I experienced my first unspoken hurt at the age of seven on a Christmas Eve. My dad came from Columbia, South Carolina with gifts for my brothers and me. Sure, I knew we lived with our grandparents, but it was something about my dad coming and leaving that caused an unheard cry in my spirit. A Question left in a young child's heart.

Another unspoken hurt was being bullied and teased because our mother drank alcohol, but if they only knew the story behind what caused this beautiful soul to turn her unspoken hurt into alcohol consumption it was to numb the pain that had impacted and imprisoned her. I believe all of them would choke on their own laughter. I encourage you to look beyond what you see. Many people are wearing masks to cover up the unheard cry. Some turn to alcohol, others to drugs, many to sex, and some even became suicidal.

Take a moment to reflect on a person that you may have encountered that you took a part of the laughter, bullying, conversation and later found out the true hurt or story behind the pain. Take a moment and reflect. Now can you write a prayer asking God to forgive you and make a sincere attempt to not judge what you do not know? Reflect on this Scripture: Matthew 7:1-2 NIV - Do not judge, or you too will be judged. For in the same way, you judge others, you will be judged, and with the measure you use, it will be measured to you.

There's also righteous judging - John 7:24 KJV says Judge not according to the appearance but judge righteous judgement. In other words, when we judge ourselves and our neighbors, our judgment must be truthful. Not what we heard from someone else about another person, or what we think, but the truth!

As for me, if the enemy had his way on the school bus that day, I might have been serving time in jail back then while riding on the bus to and from school. That evening, I kept hearing your drunken mama repeatedly from the person while others were laughing. I was drinking a soda and all I remember hearing was the sound it made when I pulled the top off and with anger, I headed to the back of the bus and that unheard cry came to the surface. We fought a good fight, but how many of you know that what the devil meant for evil God will turn into Good? Genesis 50:20 is a good lesson from Joseph when his brothers came up against him.

> ***Genesis 50:20 - You intended to harm me, but God intended it for good to accomplish what is now being done, the saving of many lives. NIV***

One last unspoken hurt that led to heart healing was the time my grandmother sent me to our neighbor's house to get a cup of flour. Little did I know that she left or wasn't at home. Her son and a friend were there so when I said, is Mrs. So and so home? He said, momma in the back. So, as I walked to the back saying Mrs. So and so, grandmama sent me for a cup of flour. But the plan of the enemy was being put in action, one locked the front door and the other the back door. The Holy Spirit gave me this uneasy feeling. As I walked back to the front, they grabbed me, and I began screaming for somebody to help me!

Well, what the enemy meant for harm (evil), God had a ram in the bush, "my saving angel" in the form of my cousin. He heard me and came knocking on the door. They opened the door as it was funny. All I know is that I ran like the wind and can't remember up to this day what happened between the run and getting home to safety or even if I ever told my grandma. But again, it became a moment of "I couldn't Hear Me Cry." Up to this day, whenever I see them, the hurt and anger will emerge. I've never approached them as an adult to tell them that they have been a part of the hurt in my life, but I forgave them and the hurt has been healed.

There have been many more unspoken hurts in my life and the fact that "I Couldn't Hear Me Cry" is the root cause of some of the actions and reactions that I have carried in my heart today. But I would love you to concentrate and meditate on this Scripture from Psalms 34:18 and write your thoughts on it. Also, write down a prayer if there is anyone or anything in your heart that you need to forgive to get to your healing.

Psalms 34:18 – The Lord is close to the brokenhearted and saves those who are crushed in Spirit. NIV

Say this Prayer with me if you can't write one of your own:

Dear Lord,

Let me turn to you for strength and peace. When I am weak, please lift me up. When I'm crushed in spirit, calm my spirits. Help me not to focus on my past hurts but to look unto you for the power to forgive, for hope and wisdom. Amen.

" Measure the size of the obstacles against the size of God. "

Beth Moore

" Our Lord never drew power from Himself, He drew it always from His Father. "

Oswald Chambers

HEALING PRAYER BOX

Write Your Own Healing Prayer.

HEALING JOURNALING PAGE

Journaling helps you to control your emotions, which in turn helps you to heal, so use this journaling page to journal how you are feeling.

HEALING JOURNALING PAGE

HEALING JOURNALING PAGE

HEALING JOURNALING PAGE

HEALING JOURNALING PAGE

Healing Affirmation

WRITE & RECITE

I am Healed

_____

_____

Anxiety The Joy Stealer

Philippians 4:6-7: *Be anxious for nothing, but in everything by prayer and supplication, with thanksgiving, let your requests be made known to God; 7 and the peace of God, which surpasses all understanding, will guard your hearts and minds through Christ Jesus. NIV*

At some point in our lives, we have experienced some form of anxiety, worry, stress, just doubting things. You look at your money and it's funny, your change looks strange, confusion in the home, children going astray, jobs demanding more and more being cooped up, this pandemic of covid – covid everywhere can you please disappear. These are just a few of the things that can cause "ANXIETY"!

Listen, I'm in my 60's now and I'm just learning how to breathe and let go of the things that are stealing my joy. And you need to do the same thing if you do not want your joy to be stolen from you. Now let's look at Philippians 4:6-7.

It's a command to be anxious about nothing. Wow, if we're going against this and doing the opposite, then we are not trusting God's promises and abilities to take care of us. Well, I've been guilty of this all too often. What about you?

Psalms 34:18 - The Lord is close to the brokenhearted and saves those who are crushed in Spirit. NIV

So how do we begin to defeat Anxiety? Well, God tells us we should pray to Him with thanksgiving and make our request known to Him. So, when we are worried, we have to pray. When we're stressed and anxious, we need to pray. Do not take your focus off God because when you do, you will begin to sink, and your focus will be on the problem. You will feel like you're drowning and can't come up for air. Can I tell you that God is bigger than what we are going through or the things our eyes can see? Look unto the hills from whence cometh your help. Psalm 121:1. God is our healer, our provider, and our everything.

Remember who you are and to whom you belong - the Great Physician, the I am that I am, Jehovah Jireh. Reflect on what Philippians 4:6-7 says to you.

Write your own prayer or repeat this prayer.

Lord here I am _____. I come before you with all my cares and burdens and I'm laying them at your feet. When I'm overwhelmed by my fears and worries, remind me of your grace, mercy, and power. Fill me with your peace as I trust you Lord. I thank you for being my hope, strength, and joy – Amen.

When I couldn't hear me Cry, now I know that God was right there with me all the time with things that were keeping me impacted and imprisoned. But what I know now is that God was waiting on me to free myself. 1st Peter 5:6, NIV: "Humble yourselves; therefore, under God's Mighty hand; that He may lift you up in honor.

I encourage you to confess whatever it is that is burdening you and be willing to leave it at the feet of Jesus. Don't take it back! I did this for a time with our son. When he first began getting into trouble, going back and forth to jail. I kept crying, blaming myself, and being his crutch, until my spiritual mom told me he was only loaned to me to be a steward over. "He belongs to God and you must give him back.

Just like a baby in your arms when you held him, now you must take that baby in your arms and hand him back over to his creator to mold him and make him as he will. Did I give and take back? Yes! But when I was fully committed, tired, broken, and couldn't take anymore, I said this prayer;

Lord it's me _____(Carolyn), please forgive me for doing only what you can do. I asked that you take _____(Jr.) and do as you will in his life. I ask that you release me from the hurt, pain, guilt, and unforgiveness I have for myself. I trust you God for you know the plans and purpose for my life and _____(Jr.). So, have he/she _____ (Jr.) is Lord, I release and let go!!!! In Jesus name – Amen.

After I did this completely, I began to feel free! I also want to say that in the end, you can find wholeness through anxiety. There's good anxiety and bad anxiety. Good anxiety is when the Holy Spirit is trying to get your attention. When things keep resurfacing and recurring and you want to do something about it, I'll tell you like the Dottie People song says: "Let Jesus lead you all the way. He's a mighty good leader, doctor, heart fixer and mind regulator!

Bad anxiety is when you become overwhelmed by a situation, circumstance, or person. You begin to lose sleep and worry about the "what ifs," your heart begins to palpitate, you seem dizzy at times, and lose your appetite. Then your primary doctor starts prescribing anxiety meds such as Xanax, Ambien, and other known drugs to calm your spirit.

I am not saying that you shouldn't get help, but you have the opportunity to choose to want to be healed and there are some goals that you can set in place for yourself to alleviate some of the stress activators in your life. Here is my go-to list:

- Cast your cares on God (Prayer)
- Mediate•Music
- Exercise, run, walk
- Diffusing essential oil
- Fruits and Veggies

Write down your feeling of how you plan to replace anxiety with victory and your go-to Scripture. I pray that by the time you finish reading this chapter, you will come to realize that God created us for His good pleasure, and we are more than conquerors through Christ Jesus!

John 10:10 (KJV): The thief cometh not, but for to steal, and to kill, and to destroy; I am come that they might have life, and that they might have it more abundantly.

The thief (Satan), (adversary), (enemy) comes to steal your finances, to kill your family relationship and destroy your hopes and dreams. But I encourage you to fight the good fight of faith, be bold and courageous. Pray without ceasing, be confident of this very thing, that He who has begun a good work in you will complete it until the day of Jesus Christ. Philippians 1:6 KJV

This is an opportunity for you to listen to that cry that's on the inside of you, waiting to be heard so that you can live that life that God has promised you. Are there going to still be challenges? Oh Yes! But you'll be better equipped to manage the anxiety.

What good fight are you going to fight to keep anxiety from stealing your joy?

HEALING PRAYER BOX

Write Your Own Healing Prayer.

HEALING JOURNALING PAGE

Journaling helps you to control your emotions, which in turn helps you to heal, so use this journaling page to journal how you are feeling.

HEALING JOURNALING PAGE

HEALING JOURNALING PAGE

HEALING JOURNALING PAGE

HEALING JOURNALING PAGE

Healing Affirmation

WRITE & RECITE

My past doesn't affect my current healed state.

_____

_____

Imprisoned by Guilt

Deuteronomy 31:8 *The Lord himself goes before you and will be with you; he will never leave you nor forsake you. Do not be afraid; do not be discouraged. NIV*

Feeling guilty can become a life journey because it's a tactic of the enemy to hold you imprisoned by your past, by mistakes, by sickness, by whatever he can throw in your path to make you feel defeated.

I remember the day my mom died (February 6, 1987). I had just gotten off from work. My mother had our children one on each knee just singing with them. Little did I know that this would be the last day I had my mom on earth with me. When I walked in, I told the children to get ready. We were going to visit grandma on John's Island. I wasn't prepared to hear my mom say, you need to stay home and rest! I said, momma, you know that I take the kids to see grandma B on the weekends.

Something quite odd happened at that moment. Our daughter pulled away saying "I don't want to" and became so clingy to my mom. Jr followed her lead. I got tired of her pulling away and told her to go get in the car. They hesitantly went. A sense of events happened in a matter of hours. She sent my stepdad to the store, cooked my brother Benjamin his last meal, washed up, curled her hair, changed clothes, laid on the bed, put her hands across her chest and slipped away from us with a smile on her face. I've never allowed myself to think beyond this point let alone write about it!

Well as we returned from visiting my mother-in-law; as we got closer home, my brother came seemingly out of nowhere, holding on to the handle of the car door. Carolyn, Momma is gone! Not prepared for what was about to rock my world forever I said, "How do you mean momma is gone?" He rambled. She just cooked my pork chops and bread; I threw the bread away. As I turned down Courland Road and got closer to where mom lived, I saw the back of the coroner's vehicle. I told my husband, what happened now?

I heard someone say, "James don't let Carolyn out of the car." I said, "What are all these people doing out here James? Well, I came to terms with reality when I saw the coroner wagon in my parent's yard (yes, my stepdad had become a father to my two brothers and me).

As I got closer and James behind me, I went up the steps and into the living room and there laid my beautiful mom. When I got closer, I said momma, the smile was so real like she was playing a trick on me, her hands still warm. I shook her over and once, twice, all I can remember screaming was OH MOMMA!

To this day I keep asking myself where my babies were? Who broke the news to them? How was my stepdad, my brothers, and my husband? I don't remember much after that because my aunt and uncle had to be the ones that did everything up until the services. I fell into a deep depression, guilt, and alcohol. I began taking Valium and Darvon just to not feel the pain and the loss. Nobody, nobody knew how I felt. But one day I came to my senses. I had a long *bout with what they now call OPIOIDS.* Even a longer battle with alcohol.

I was tired of being sick from drinking, tired of feeling alone, tired of putting up a front and wearing masks that started to be seen through by everyone. I had a husband, daughter, and son that needed me healthy and whole, so I began my path to healing.

In John 4:2-6 (NKJV), Jesus asked the man lying at the pool for thirty-eight years, "do you want to be healed?" Well, I wanted to be healed from alcohol and from the pills. I wanted to remove the mask and praying about "At the cross, at the cross where I first saw the light and live an authentic, productive, and purposeful life. I tried on my own, but the guilt of the loss of my mom, my children's grandma, and my husband's friend (His mother-in-love) couldn't allow me. I couldn't do it on my own anymore. I needed help. I heard my grandma singing and the burdens of my heart rolled away. It was there 'by Faith' I received my sight and now I am happy all day."

I wanted that kind of freedom. I cried out to God to remove the thorns! Tears streamed from my eyes uncontrollably. I was in my car one morning on the way to work when I had a conversation with God. God knew that I was chasing after Him, and He heard my despairing cry and suddenly I was made whole. Unaware that He took the taste, desire, pain, and guilt all away that morning. I can say just like that song that I'm free, praise the Lord, I'm free, no longer bound, and no more chains holding me.

> " What may seem defeat to us may be victory to Him "
>
> *C. H. Spurgeon*

All of us face life-altering guilt, pain, and circumstances that leave us overwhelmed with a feeling of defeat, but God is right there through the difficult times. If we call out to Him, He will answer.

> The next time you are hurt, you feel guilt or disappointment, don't give up. Just be patient and let God remind you He's still in control.
>
> *Max Lucado*

Deuteronomy 31:8 (ESV). It is the Lord who goes before you. He will be with you; He will not leave you or forsake you. Do not fear or be dismayed.

I've had many things in my life that held me imprisoned for a season. But I'm now equipped with the lessons I learned and the experience to fight off anything that impacted me to the point of defeat.

Take the time to reflect and write about anything that may have impacted you past or present that you need the Lord to fix for you.

Let Deuteronomy 31:8 become a part of your spirit when you feel defeated and alone or find a verse and write it here.

I want to encourage you and remind you what Psalm 34:19 says (NIV); Many are the afflictions of the righteous; but out of them all the Lord will deliver them.

Trust and believe, take accountable steps to regain your peace and Joy. You are not going to be exempt from the attack of the enemy but know that God's wisdom will help you to escape the snares and tangles of the setup and plans of the enemy.

After you've read these scriptures, quotes and prayers; begin to walk into your destiny of freedom from the impact of guilt and the bondage it had on you. Put in place some strategic plans for finding wholeness through brokenness. I'd love to give you a few and, in the space, provided you can add and implement more steps of your own.

- Get into God's Word daily.
- Set up times and space for meditation.
- Listen to Praise and Worship or calming and relaxing instrumental music.
- Soak in a bath burning scented candles.
- Diffuse essential oils like Lavender, Frankincense, orange or lemon.
- Drink a nice tea, your favorite coffee or latte.
- Exercise or walk.
- Eat healthy well-balanced meals to include fruits, veggies and water.

Yes, you may have been impacted by guilt, but know that 2nd Corinthians 10:4 (NIV) tells us that the weapons of our warfare are not of the flesh but have divine power to destroy strongholds. You see, the weapons we use are not worldly against this attack of guilt which is a warfare. We cannot conquer guilt on our own, or with a carnal or fleshly mindset. We need to proclaim what God said along with being submissive and letting our request known unto Him believing that He (God) will give us His strength and Godly Wisdom to guide us to total freedom.

HEALING PRAYER BOX

Write Your Own Healing Prayer.

HEALING JOURNALING PAGE

Journaling helps you to control your emotions, which in turn helps you to heal, so use this journaling page to journal how you are feeling.

HEALING JOURNALING PAGE

HEALING JOURNALING PAGE

HEALING JOURNALING PAGE

HEALING JOURNALING PAGE

Healing Affirmation

WRITE & RECITE

I've let go of my pain and I am healed.

_____

_____

The Power of Forgiveness
(It Frees You!!)

There will be many who will have their own thoughts and opinions of what forgiveness is but whatever the reason you choose and the way you do it, it matters. Forgiveness does not mean that you won't think about what happened to you, with you, or against someone else. When you truly forgive someone, yourself, the situation or circumstances, it FREES YOU! Look at this verse of scripture. Read it aloud.

Daniel 9:9 - The Lord our God is merciful and forgiving, even though we have rebelled against Him (NIV). What word do you see here that shows us the love of our forgiving Father? Yes, His mercifulness, even though we have sinned against Him, others, even ourselves, he still forgives. We are carnal beings, but we can still have spiritual thoughts.

I struggled to forgive myself through decisions, mistakes, and choices that I made. Not knowing then what I know now that God is a forgiving God! I've learned to accept the past and plan for my future. What can I say to you that will help you through the impact of forgiveness? Well, read and listen carefully to what this verse in Philippians says to us - Philippians 3:13-14 (NKJV) - Brethren, I do not count myself to have [a] apprehended; but one thing I do, forgetting those things which are behind and reaching forward to those things which are ahead, 14 I press toward the goal for the prize of the upward call of God in Christ Jesus.

The very things in life that cause roadblocks and keep us from forgiving ourselves, others, choices, and mistakes are not the ones we see through the windshield; they are the ones that we see in the rearview mirror. We find it hard to accept or let go of the PAST. "Painful- Anxiety-Stressful - Tension."

" Shake the dust from your past, and move forward in His promises. "

Kay Arthur

" We can't just put our past behind us. We've got to put our past in front of God "

Beth Moore

"Our yesterdays present irreparable things to us; it is true that we have lost opportunities that will never return, but God can transform this destructive anxiety into a constructive thoughtfulness for the future. Let the past sleep, but let it sleep in the bosom of Christ. Leave the irreparable past in His hands, and step out into the irresistible future with Him "

Oswald Chambers

Listening to unforgiveness cannot change what happened yesterday, Crying can't change the past, nor regrets. Worrying, bitterness, or anger can't change what has happened, but we can change the outcome. List below some opportunities that may present themselves and steps you can take to forgive yourself or someone else.

_____
_____
_____
_____
_____
_____
_____
_____
_____
_____
_____
_____
_____
_____
_____

Remember in the beginning what I said. Forgiveness frees you!

I hope that you can begin to feel the freedom and live the joyous life that God has planned for you to live. It is not meant for you to give up your peace of mind, to feel guilty about choices, decisions, or mistakes. This life is not for you to give your power over to anyone, but to accept the power of the living God that is within you and to allow the Holy Spirit to lead, guide, direct and instruct you to all understanding – the understanding is that Jesus Christ is the same yesterday, today and forever. Hebrews-13:8 (NLT)

Start basking in the love of Christ, taking Him at His words and believing in His promises. He promised that He will never leave us or forsake us. But because I couldn't hear me crying, I allowed myself to become impacted and imprisoned and even though I knew His words then, it didn't apply to my heart then as it does now. Oh, if you can only believe in your heart that God will remove the past hurts, the spirit of unforgiveness, the worries and anxieties if you apply the word to your life and live it out by faith and trust God to do the rest.

If God is in it, you can win it. For you give yourself to God, to do the work that needs to be done in mind, body, and soul. Romans 8:35, 37 (NKJV) says who shall separate us from the love of Christ? Shall tribulations, or distress, or persecution, or sword? Yet in all these things we are more than conquerors through Him who loved us.

And when His word really gets to the core of you becoming free, you can confidently say without another thought what Romans 8:38-39 tells us (NASB). For I am convinced that neither death, nor life, nor angels nor principalities, nor things present, nor things to come, nor powers, nor heights, nor depth, nor any other created thing, will be able to separate us from the love of God, which is in Christ Jesus our Lord.

Let Us Pray

Father God, let me learn to live in the present and not the past, let me count my blessings, and not my pain. Give me the knowledge and wisdom to be thankful for every opportunity to forgive myself or someone else. Help me to accept what was, let me give thanks for what is and let me have faith to see the goodness of the Lord and the promise of eternal life with you – Amen. I hope this prayer has lifted some of the adversities that have caused you to be stagnant, feeling bound, overcast with burdens and cares over you that you thought would imprison and hold you captive. Our God is awesome and as 1st Peter 5:7 (NIV) says – We should cast all our cares (Anxiety) on Him because He cares for us. There's no worry or concern that God cannot take away. We just must trust His word completely and stand on the promises of God.

Below are some ways you can forgive yourself. Check your emotions; are you angry, hurt, casting blame, feel like crying or isolated?

- Acknowledge the guilt you're feeling
- Apologize to anyone you may have hurt
- Admit your mistakes
- Be patient in the process
- Stop trying to change other people

Oh, let me define "Forgiveness" for you. It's a deliberate decision to let go of feelings of anger, resentment, and retribution toward someone who you believe has wronged you or you have wronged.

Another thing I would like to say is, it's okay to forgive others and love from a distance. It's okay to accept God's forgiveness for yourself and move forward with a guilt-free conscience. It's an absolutely amazing and peaceful feeling to know that your self-love and self-care depend on your self-worth.

Take advantage of the space provided below to write down a few things that you will do to create a more rewarding, rejuvenating, gracious, and joyful part of your life.

It's time that we come to grips that unforgiveness holds us in bondage and it's a trap of the enemy. It comes to steal, to kill and to destroy. Let's focus on the promise that He comes to give us life and to the abundance filled with hope, faith, inspiration and to the full.

In the end, unforgiveness will consume you mentally, physically, and spiritually. Most definitely, you cannot be in a full relationship with God if you are unwilling to forgive. Matthew 6:14-15 (NIV) says "If you forgive others of their transgression, your Heavenly Father will also forgive you, but if you do not forgive others, then your Father will not forgive your transgressions."

Personal Comment: Do This! Make a list of everyone that has hurt you, or you have hurt and ask God to help you to forgive them and forgive yourself. Be obedient as you pray to God for His will to be done.

"Forgiveness Frees You"

HEALING PRAYER BOX

Write Your Own Healing Prayer.

HEALING JOURNALING PAGE

Journaling helps you to control your emotions, which in turn helps you to heal, so use this journaling page to journal how you are feeling.

HEALING JOURNALING PAGE

HEALING JOURNALING PAGE

HEALING JOURNALING PAGE

HEALING JOURNALING PAGE

Healing Affirmation

WRITE & RECITE

**I am strong and
I am a survivor.**

_____

_____

Taking Care of You in Uncertain, Unexpected and Trying Times

Listen, the most important thing you can do for yourself is to take care of yourself. And all through the Bible, the word of God tells us how to do it. But this scripture from Philippians 4:6-7 (KJV) is my favorite. It says "And the peace of God which passeth all understanding; shall keep your hearts and minds through Christ Jesus. Guarding your heart means allowing that love in and letting God be your comfort. In uncertain, unexpected, and trying times, our heart goes through all kinds of emotions. You cry, you praise, there's joy, compassion, hurt and pain but in all phases of these life-changing times, we must take care of ourselves physically, mentally, emotionally and spiritually.

I love the way John 14:1-3 (KJV) puts it: 1 - let not your heart be troubled; ye believe in God, believe also in me. 2 In my father's house are many mansions, if it were not so, I would have told you so, 3 I go to prepare a place for you, and if I go and prepare a place for you, I will come again and receive you unto myself. That where I am there ye may be also.

As believers, our journey to self-care and self-love begins with trusting God. Have faith and keep holding on. Keep going even when the rubber meets the road so to speak. We all face situations at times that leave us drained, tired and impacted but we have to get to the point and make up our minds to fight the good fight of faith.

1st Timothy 6:12 (KJV) says Keeping a good mindset, doing the things that will keep us healthy in mind, body and soul. I love this quote by **C. H. Spurgeon:** *What may seem defeat to us may be Victory to Him.* If you are finding it hard taking the time to take care of yourself, perhaps it's time to ask yourself some questions:

1. *What does God say about my health?*
2. *What does God want me to learn about good health and my soul prospering?*
3. *What steps or care plan does God have in place for me?*

When you go to Him in prayer, listen for His voice and write your answers here.

_____

_____

_____

_____

_____

_____

Remember in taking care of "YOU," there are hidden opportunities and potential for your personal and spiritual growth.

" If your hopes are being disappointed, just know it means that they are being purified. "

Oswald Chambers

In your self-care journey know that

> " The next time you're disappointed don't panic, don't give up just be patient and let God remind you He's still in control "
>
> *Max Lucado*

Begin to see yourself as transformed. God stands at the door ready, and He wants you to call on Him for a renewed, refreshed, and regenerated life. Are you ready for a new beginning in taking care of you? I'm glad you said "YES." Fix your heart and mind toward God in prayer and God's word and find out what He says about you. Find a good support system of fellow believers and let the creator; the one who made you and knows all about you begin to make you over and all things will become new.

God is concerned about every area of your life. Let this quote by **Annie Graham Lutz** resonate with you. It says, "In the midst of the pressure and the heat, I am confident His hand is on my life, developing my faith until I display the glory that pleases Him!"

Reflect on this Scripture and Journal any thoughts you may have that resonate with it. You'll find a blessed assurance and peace of mind.

Isaiah 43:2 (NIV)

When you pass through the waters, I will be with you; and when you pass through the rivers, they will not sweep over you. When you walk through the fire, you will not be burned; the flames will not set you ablaze.

Speaking about taking care of us! This promise right here should cause us to get our praise on! It does not say "IF," it says when. So, we will certainly go through some stuff before we come out of the waters, rivers, and fire.

Let Us Pray

Dear Father, the Creator of all things that are good and perfect, thank you for taking care of me in uncertain times. Thank you for knowing my emotions, my thoughts, my reactions and for keeping me from day to day. For strengthening me when I'm weak and building me up when I'm torn down. For being the lifter of my head. Help me to daily walk with you, talk with you, and listen for the Holy Spirit's guidance, and instruction.
In Jesus Name –Amen.

Journal Your feelings about Isaiah 43:2 from above

What are some steps that you are going to implement in your day to continue or start your own care plan?
I couldn't hear me cry until my body started to respond to the things that I was neglecting to give it! Sleep, exercise, proper diet, and more importantly water.

This Section is for you to journal Scriptures that bring you Hope, Faith, and Peace.
For example,
I can do ALL things through Christ Jesus who strengthens me.

Philippians 4:13 NIV

It's okay to Say "No"

It was an unheard cry of mine for a long time. And I felt so guilty and thought of all the reasons. I should go back and say "Yes" and then, I begin to get drained in body, mind, and spirit! I was fond of saying "Yes" when I should have said "No" and leaving it at that without any explanations. Part of taking care of yourself is saying No! ; Eventually you'll stop feeling like a crutch for people or being overwhelmed about things to do and places to go.

Go ahead and say "No" ……. Now write down some things that you've been saying yes to that could have been a "No" and still had good end results.

Remember The Verse from John 14:1-3

Let not your heart be troubled, believe that God will order our steps and direct our paths. No good thing will He withhold from us, if we delight ourselves in Him and surrender our body, mind, and soul to Him. He already knows what we need but He's waiting on us to use the measure of faith that He gave us.

I'm reminiscing on my first book, "At the Foot of the Cross." How God had to literally lay me down to get my attention. The heart surgery I had, showed me that my family had to do what they had to do without "this caretaker" taking care of everyone, worrying about everyone, believing that it couldn't get done if I wasn't there to help.

My self-care was beginning, and He wanted my attention. He wanted me to realize that I was trying to do what only He could do. I was putting my hands into what He already ordained. So, He laid me down at the cross to show me that I have taken on all of this.

Why are you trying to carry it? It's a burden and it's affecting your health, your peace, and your wholeness.

I saw your need, but you didn't hear the cry.

Our Unheard Cry of Grief

I couldn't understand why two weeks turned into a month without writing or Journaling. I call it writer's block. I was having many dreams about my mother, dad, stepdad, and Uncle Dan but I never considered the fact that they were preparing me for a departure, loss or trauma. They were preparing me for an unheard cry that will impact me and my family for the rest of our lives.

It was April 22, 2021. I was knocked off my feet and could not accept the news that my oldest brother had died. All I could remember was repeating No, No, No, No! I don't know how many times. My co-workers knew I had a heart condition, so they quickly did all the things they knew had to be done for the safety of my health and to each of you I am so grateful.

Even as I'm writing, the tears and the palpitations are beginning. My brother was hit by several cars. I heard of the fatality on 526 and it being shut down but my brother. He was the liveliest soul anyone could meet. Fun-loving, smart, artistic, and will do anything for you. Even though we have laid him to rest, we still are looking for him to pop up, but we know it's an unheard cry - he has lived his life here on earth. He had an unheard cry, but God answered it his way and I am now at peace knowing he is physically, emotionally, spiritually, and mentally healed.

But one thing about his cry is that I'm living lessons through his life. He didn't hold grudges; he laughed daily, told you how he felt, loved the Lord, loved singing, walked daily, and was carefree. But even though I misunderstood what he was going through (isolation and dependency), the enemy impacted and imprisoned his life. He has left a legacy behind. You cannot judge the book by the cover because you cannot tell anyone's story except your own. But while living, I encourage each and every one of you to lie the dash between life and death and listen to the unheard cries that God is trying to bring to the surface in our lives.

- Learn to accept the things that you can change and change them
- Do unto others as you have them do unto you
- Pray without ceasing
- Love without conditions Give to be a blessings
- Live on purpose
- Keep the Faith
- Keep your eyes on God
- Hold your hand out to help a person when they're down
- Feed your spirit

- Forgive without malice
- Be free to be you
- Your character births integrity
- Your attitude will elevate your altitude

I am missing my brother daily, but as Chris told a family member in the spirit. "It was senseless, but it was fair," I'm in a beautiful place. I am going to see you again dear brother. But the impact you left on us will be displayed and lived by every chapter in this book.

- Yes, as Psalm 34:18 says - God is near to the brokenhearted, and He saves those of a contrite spirit. Our hurts God will heal.
- Our anxiety we can cast on God - 1st Peter 5:7 (NIV)
- The guilt will be replaced with peace that surpasses all understanding - Matthew 7:24-27 (NKJV)
- We'll be able to forgive to free us - Matthew 6:12-14
- We'll learn to care for ourselves the way God intends 3rd John 2
- We know that weeping may endure for a night but Joy Cometh in the morning light - Psalm 30:5 (KJV)

I pray that this book/journal blesses you and that you use it to face unheard cries and the weapons that want to impact and hold you imprisoned. Open this book whenever you feel hurt, alone, bitter, or unloved. Use it to help someone else to face feelings that have been locked up inside for so long. But most of all, I've shared my heart about how I am living beyond my unheard cries, and you can too.

Blessings,

HEALING PRAYER BOX

Write Your Own Healing Prayer.

HEALING JOURNALING PAGE

Journaling helps you to control your emotions, which in turn helps you to heal, so use this journaling page to journal how you are feeling.

_____

_____

_____

_____

_____

_____

_____

_____

_____

_____

_____

_____

_____

_____

_____

_____

HEALING JOURNALING PAGE

HEALING JOURNALING PAGE

HEALING JOURNALING PAGE

HEALING JOURNALING PAGE

Healing Affirmation

WRITE & RECITE

**I have healed all
past trauma.**

_____

_____

Conclusion:

"The most beautiful part of you is you!"

With Jesus on your side and you reaching out to Him all things are possible to those who believe. **Mark 9:23**

Impacted But Not Imprisoned

Carolyn Blake is affectionately known as "The Impacter." Carolyn Empowers, Encourages, and Impact women to live beyond life's adversities through Hope. Faith. Inspiration.

Carolyn is the author of At the Foot of the Cross, a story of her encounter with the Lord. How He (the Lord) led her to defeat the attack of the enemy through Faith, Hope, and Prayer.

Carolyn hosts a weekly podcast to encourage her tribe of Faith-based women to live their best lives even when anxiety comes to attack them.

As the Visionary of Impacted But Not Imprisoned, LLC Carolyn has Hosted two amazing spirit-led, spirit-filled conferences where women came together in a safe environment to give testimonies, to receive resources and information, and to be poured into by other women that found wholeness through their brokenness.

Carolyn has been interviewed by Author and life coach Kimberly Boone, by The Logan Power Show, and by Women Destined for Greatness. Carolyn, has surrounded herself with mentors to empower and enrich her Ministry. Carolyn's life's motto is: "If I can help somebody along the way, then my living shall not be in vain."

Her favorite Scripture is: Psalm 23

You can connect with Carolyn on Facebook, Twitter, Instagram, LinkedIn, and YouTube or on her website www.impactedbutnotimprisoned.com

Interested in Writing and or Publishing a Book?
Contact Dr. Synovia @ www.a2zbookspublishing.net

www.ingramcontent.com/pod-product-compliance
Lightning Source LLC
Chambersburg PA
CBHW061204070526
44579CB00010B/123